Presented To

_____

By

_____

Occasion

_____

Date

_____

Deep Blue Bible Storybook
Miracles of Jesus

No part of this work may be reproduced or transmitted in any form or by any means, electronic or mechanical, including photocopying and recording, or by any information storage or retrieval system, except as may be expressly permitted by the 1976 Copyright Act or by permission in writing from the publisher. Requests for permission should be submitted in writing to: Rights and Permissions, The United Methodist Publishing House, 2222 Rosa L. Parks Blvd., PO Box 280988, Nashville, TN 37228-0988; faxed to 615-749-6128; or submitted via e-mail to *permissions@abingdonpress.com*.

Co-written by Kerry Blackwood, Daphna Flegal, and Brittany Sky; with special thanks to Elizabeth F. Caldwell
Editors: Erin Floyd, Brittany Sky
Designer: Matthew Allison

Cover Art (Deep Blue Kids) by: Tim Moen (Character Design), Jesse Griffin (3D Artist), Julio Medina (3D Artist), Eric M. Mikula (Facial Rigging), and Christopher Slavik (Layout Artist); Background: Four Story Creative.

Internal Art: Four Story Creative; Deep Blue Kids illustrations by Tim Moen, Jesse Griffin, Julio Medina, Eric M. Mikula, and Christopher Slavik.

ISBN: 9781501840630
PACP10512069-01

17 18 19 20 21 22 23 24 25 26—10 9 8 7 6 5 4 3 2 1

Printed in the United States of America.

Contents

Hi, friends! We're glad you are here to dive deep with us into God's Word. We'll have adventures and learn fun facts on our journey.

The Bible is more than just a big book; it's a gift to us from God! It's also a gift to us from many people. It took hundreds of years and thousands of people to bring us this gift. And like all good gifts, the Bible is meant to be opened, explored, and enjoyed. It's our hope that you will learn more about God, the Bible, Jesus, faith, and how it all fits into life today.

Matthew

The first four books of the New Testament, the Gospels, tell exciting stories about Jesus. The Book of Matthew is about the kingdom of God. Many of the miracles performed in Matthew show us what God's kingdom might be like.

Tips for **Adults**

The Book of Matthew was written at the end of the first century by an anonymous writer. Church tradition identified the writer as Matthew, but we don't know for sure. We do know that the author teaches the audience that Jesus is the Christ and the interpreter of the Jewish Scriptures. The author teaches us that Jesus came so people could experience God's kingdom.

The Man in the Synagogue
Matthew 12:9-14

Jesus and his friends went to the synagogue—a place where Jewish people worshipped God. A man with a hurt hand was there.

The leaders at the synagogue wanted to get Jesus in trouble, so they asked him a question about God's rules.

"Do God's rules allow a person to heal on the day of rest?"

Jesus answered, "If your sheep fell into a pit on the day of rest, wouldn't you get the sheep out of the pit? People are more important than sheep. God's rules say to do what is good on the day of rest."

Jesus said to the man with the hurt hand, "Give me your hand." The man stretched out his hand, and his hand was healed.

How do you think the man with the hurt hand felt?

Mark

The Book of Mark is an action-packed book. It begins with Jesus' baptism by John the Baptist and ends with Jesus' resurrection. In the middle, it teaches us about the healings and miracles Jesus performed.

Tips for
Adults

The Book of Mark doesn't say anything about Jesus' birth, instead, it jumps right in to the ministry of Jesus' life. The Book of Mark was the first Gospel book written and was used as a source to write the Books of Matthew and Luke. Mark is the shortest of the Gospels, and highlights the healings and miracles Jesus performed.

The Four Friends
Mark 2:1-12

Jesus went back to Capernaum. People heard that he was there and came to his home. There were so many people at the house that there was not space to even go inside.

Jesus was teaching the people when four friends arrived carrying a man on a mat. The man was paralyzed, so he could not walk. It was so crowded, the friends could not carry him through the crowd.

The four friends did not give up! They carried the man who was paralyzed to the roof. They tore through the roof of the home and lowered their friend on his mat to Jesus.

How did the man who could not walk feel? What does this story teach us about being a friend?

Jesus saw their faith and said, "You are forgiven! Get up and walk."

Right away, the man picked up his mat and walked out in front of everybody! Everyone was amazed. They praised God.

Jesus Calms the Storm
Mark 4:35-41

Jesus had been teaching the crowds. At the end of the day, Jesus said to the disciples, "Let's go across to the other side of the lake." So they left on a boat.

Big, strong winds began blowing the water! The disciples were scared, but not Jesus. He was sleeping in the back of the boat.

The disciples woke Jesus up and said, "Teacher, don't you care that we are drowning?"

Jesus got up and told the wind to be still and silent. The wind settled down, and everything was calm.

Jesus asked the disciples, "Why are you afraid? Don't you have faith yet?"

The disciples were filled with wonder because of what Jesus had done. They looked at each other and said, "Who is this man? The wind and the sea obey him."

Jairus's Daughter
Mark 5:21-24, 35-43

When Jesus arrived at the lakeshore, a crowd of people were waiting for him. Everyone crowded around Jesus.

Jairus, an important leader, came rushing up to Jesus. He fell down at Jesus' feet. "Jesus!" cried Jairus. "My daughter is really sick. Please come and touch her so she will get better."

Jesus and his disciples followed Jairus to his home. While they were walking, some of Jairus's friends stopped them. Jesus and Jairus stopped walking to listen to Jairus's friends. "Your daughter is dead," said the friends. "Jesus doesn't need to come."

But Jesus said, "No. Don't be afraid. Keep trusting." Jesus took two of his helpers and went to Jairus's daughter. She was lying on a bed.

Her mother stood beside the bed, crying. "Why are you crying?" asked Jesus. "The child is not dead. She is only sleeping."

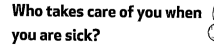

Who takes care of you when you are sick?

Then Jesus took the girl's hand. "Little girl," Jesus said, "get up!" And the little girl got up and began to walk around!

Bartimaeus Shouts to Jesus
Mark 10:46-52

Jesus and his crowd of followers had traveled to Jericho. They were on their way out of town when they noticed a man named Bartimaeus sitting beside the road. Bartimaeus was blind, so he could not see. Bartimaeus was begging for someone to help him. When Bartimaeus heard that Jesus was there, he began to shout, "Jesus! Please help me!"

The crowd told Bartimaeus to be quiet, but he just shouted louder, "Jesus! Please help me!"

Jesus heard Bartimaeus and told Bartimaeus to come to him. Bartimaeus jumped up and came to Jesus.

Jesus asked Bartimaeus what he needed. The blind man said, "Teacher, I want to see!"

Jesus said, "Go! Your faith has healed you!" At once, Bartimaeus was able to see and he followed Jesus.

What do you think it would be like to see for the first time?

Luke

The Book of Luke teaches us about what Jesus did in the world. Jesus preached the good news, healed people's minds and bodies, and showed everyone he met God's big love. Jesus' miracles show how much God loves all people!

Tips for **Adults**

The author of Luke also wrote the Book of Acts. The author wanted to give an organized narrative account of what happened during Jesus' life and what happened with the first believers to the early Christian groups.

This book explains Jesus' mission in the world. Jesus said he came "to preach good news to the poor, to proclaim release to the prisoners and recovery of sight to the blind, to liberate the oppressed" (Luke 4:18).

Jesus Heals
Luke 4:38-44

esus walked from the city of Nazareth, his hometown, to the city of Capernaum. While he was in the city, he taught the people about God's love.

Then Jesus went with Peter to Peter's home. Peter's mother-in-law was sick. She had a high fever.

Jesus bent over Peter's mother-in-law and spoke to her. Immediately, her fever went away.

Peter's mother-in-law felt much better, so she got up and served everyone.

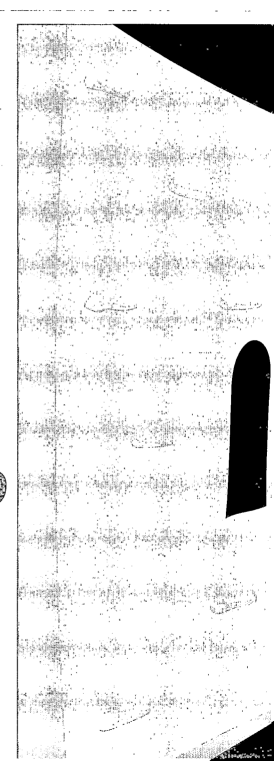

At the end of the day, many people brought their family and friends who were sick to Jesus. Jesus touched them and healed them.

Then Jesus went to another city to teach the people about God's love.

Why did many people bring their friends and family who were sick to see Jesus?

Ten Lepers

Luke 17:11-19

esus was walking to Jerusalem, and on the way he saw ten men. The men were very sick. The men had a skin illness called leprosy. The men were not allowed to be around anyone but each other.

The men saw Jesus, and they yelled out to him, "Jesus, please heal us! We are ten very sick men!"

Jesus saw the ten men. The he said, "Go show yourselves to the priests."

The ten men turned around and started walking to see the priests, but on the way, something happened. The ten men were healed! All the spots on their skin went away!

One of the men who was healed turned around and ran back to Jesus. The man said, "Jesus, thank you for healing me!"

Jesus asked, "Why did only one of you return? Weren't all ten men healed?" Jesus said to the man, "Your faith has made you well."

? How do you think the ten men felt when they were sick? Why is it important to say thank you?

John

The story of Jesus in the Book of John is different from the other Gospels. The author of John tells the miracle stories of Jesus using beautiful words and images. These miracles teach us about Jesus.

Tips for Adults

The Book of John was probably the last of the four Gospels—Matthew, Mark, Luke, and John—written. The author is unknown, though tradition says that John, son of Zebedee, wrote the book. The Book of John focuses more on who Jesus is, the Son of God, and teaches less about God's kingdom. John teaches us that Jesus was "the Word" who was with God at the very beginning.

The Man by the Pool
John 5:1-17

One day Jesus walked to a place where there was a pool of swirling water. Many sick people visited the pool because they thought the water would make them well.

Sitting by the pool was a man who had not been able to walk for many years.

Jesus saw the man and asked, "Do you want to get well?"

The man said, "Jesus, I want to get in the pool when the water is swirling, but I need someone to lift me in. Someone else always gets in before anyone can help me."

Jesus said, "Pick up your mat and walk!"

Immediately, the man got up! He picked up his mat and walked away from the pool.

Jesus healed the man on a sabbath day, a day of rest. On sabbath days, nobody was supposed to do any work, including healing sick people.

When the Jewish leaders heard that Jesus had healed the man on the sabbath day, they became very angry.

How do you think the man felt when he was able to get up and walk?

Jesus knew the Jewish leaders would get angry, but Jesus helped people whenever he could, even on sabbath days.

A Boy's Lunch
John 6:1-15

One sunny day, Jesus and his disciples crossed the Sea of Galilee. A huge crowd followed them. The crowd had heard about Jesus' stories and about the miracles he was performing. The crowd hoped to see the power of God through Jesus.

The crowd followed Jesus and the disciples up into the mountains. Jesus looked out into the crowd and said to his friend, Philip, "There have to be over five thousand people here, and they haven't eaten anything. Where can we buy food for these people?" Philip knew they could not afford to buy food for that many people.

Another disciple, Andrew, noticed a boy in the crowd who had five loaves of bread and two fish. Andrew brought the boy to Jesus.

"If you think it will help," said the boy, "I will share my food."

So Jesus took the bread and fish, and said, "Dear God, thank you for our blessings." Jesus broke the bread and fish, and began passing it out to the people.

Everyone in the crowd ate until each person was full. Jesus performed a miracle! "Pick up what is left," Jesus said. There were twelve baskets of food left!

Jesus cares about full bellies, and so should we. How can you help others get enough food to eat?